RELAX
Wine Down & Color

A Great Way To Relieve STRESS
&
Calm Your Mind

Written by: **Tanasha S. Allwood**

Published by: **Graphic Lion Media**

Illustrated by: **Buzzed Art Nite, LLC**

Copyright © 2017 Tanasha S. Allwood
Published by Graphic Lion Media
www.graphiclionmedia.com

Printed in the United States of America

ISBN: 0692854894
ISBN-13: 978-0692854891

Dedication

This book is dedicated to my one and only son Jordan, I know we have had our ups and downs but through it all I would not change a thing. Those are our experiences that we both have made it through and shaped us into who we are today. I love you son with all my heart and I encourage you to always pursue your DREAMS. It's never too late and YOU CAN be anything your heart desires, just remember to put God 1st!

A very special dedication to my # 1 cheerleader, Andrea. You are a beautiful woman inside and out and you truly have a heart of gold. Thank you so much for always providing a non-judgmental, empathic ear whenever I needed to just TALK. I love you sis with all my heart. Don't ever change.

To my dear mother who's encouraging words of wisdom always seem to ring through even when I didn't want to hear it. Thank you mom for telling me to keep pushing forward and not to give up and for cooking me some fried catfish or fried chicken wings with a side of fries to cheer me up when I needed it most. I love you.

To my aunt Laura for always sharing and liking my posts on social media and being a great supporter of everything I do, even from millions of miles away. I love you Auntie.

To my honey. You know who you are and I love you so much. You know me inside and out and have been there for me even on days when I wanted to give up. Our partnership means a lot and I appreciate you being in my world and I value what we have together.

To my Jaxx, man I wish you could talk. You are the best buddy a girl could have. You are always so HAPPY to see me and I just love you to absolute pieces.

To my brother Stanley, just like mom always tells me; just keep pushing forward. All of your hard work will soon pay off and I hope to be an inspiration to you. Take care of your health and know that big sis will ALWAYS have your back! I love you man.

To my dearest Bobby, whom I knew nothing about until the age of 17, and then decided just 4 short years ago to build a relationship with you after it was too late. I hope you are smiling down on "Yours Truly" and proud of my accomplishments. Love your one and only.

And most importantly, to my GOD for giving me life and everything that goes along with it. By drawing closer to you, I discovered my purpose and I am so thankful to do your work and bless and inspire others with my talents. Without you, I know none of this would be possible.

CONTENTS

Acknowledgments

Many Thanks to:

Pastor Thomas Bessix of The Greater Works Church in Lewisville, TX for helping me to stay grounded in HIS Word.

My business mentors at WiNGS, SCORE, and the local Texas SBDC offices for your constant encouragement to keep going forward and reminding me to celebrate my successes along the way, no matter how big or small.

Chuck at CODEGraphfix for assisting me with the illustration of the images in this book. Not sure what I would have done without your services.

My contract artists at Buzzed Art Nite: Nychelle Else, Josh Clay, Tasia Teague, Ana Camila, Anita Mays, Adrienne McMillon, JJ Taylor, and Dawneisha Taylor. Each of you have a very special gift and I am forever grateful to be working with such amazing artists. Your work inspires me to do what I do and I thank you.

My VIP clients at BUZZED ART NITE. Thank you all for your continued support by being in attendance at all of my past events, (especially you Connie Derrough) the first to purchase new products, your constant positive feedback and areas for improvement. I am excited to give each of you a free copy of my new book.

The City of Dallas for allowing me to become a vendor and provide my services to SENIORS who often times need a way to relax and have something fun and new to do.

Secret Bridgewater for believing in me and what I am trying to accomplish and for helping me to think of new, fun and creative ways to market my new book.

All my family and friends spread out across the world. Thank you for staying connected with me on social media. Especially you dad. Your support is truly appreciated.

Les Brown and Gerry Roberts for providing the Get MOTIVATED and Publish a Book & Grow RICH seminars. It was those seminars that my suppressed passion had been re-ignited inside of me to finally start and finish my first book. The tips I learned by attending that class were truly invaluable.

Heatron Manufacturing, Johnson County Government, and Direct General Insurance, our mutual agreements played a critical role in my life journey today.

Lesley Tyrone Spencer-Griggs for your introduction to Eric Bettis, the Owner of Graphic Lion Media and to Graphic Lion Media for your assistance in helping me to bring this book project to life. Thank You!

About the Author

Two year ago I stepped out on FAITH and started my business called Buzzed Art Nite. It's a mobile sip & paint company located in Dallas Fort-Worth where I teach all walks of life who have an appreciation for FUN, contemporary, pop-cultured artwork, how to Laugh, RELAX, Wine Down & Paint. Buzzed Art Nite has been featured on Good Morning Texas-WFAA Channel 8 and The Morning Show with NBC DFW Channel 5. It has been my hope to inspire other people like myself that may have struggled with bouts of depression and how to relieve their stress and anxiety of the day.

Coloring as well as painting are in fact a form of Art Therapy. They are a great way to express yourself and they both help to RELAX you and improve your overall mood and mental state of mind. Lord knows that throughout my many dark days, I found it pretty overwhelming to cope with life and at one point even considered throwing in the towel and ending it all. However, it was HE who said to me, "Have FAITH and follow your Passion". "For I gave that desire to you for a reason".

Therefore, after allowing myself to get still and hearing HIS voice, I decided to write this adult coloring book. The book itself is a great compliment to my business. For those that may not be able to attend one of my unique art experiences, it truly is my pleasure to bring more awareness to the concept of art therapy and have you experience it by coloring some of the very images that we paint in my Buzzed Art Nite sessions. For I believe, that by doing so, you too will be blessed, inspired, feel more calm and have found a new way to relieve your stress and anxiety.

I am originally from a small town in Kansas called Leavenworth. Until about the age of 16, I was raised a military brat, traveling all over the world, having lived in places such as Hawaii, Kentucky, Georgia, Germany, Michigan, Missouri and Kansas. I relocated to Dallas in 2014 and fell in love with the city. I have two younger siblings, a 5-year-old yorkie and one teenage son. I absolutely admire everything art and I consider myself to be a humbled, driven, creative, motivated and determined individual. My CORE Values are transparency, perseverance, FAITH, FUN, laughter trust and dependability and it is my hope that you will find some value and inspiration in this book and use it as a tool to assist you on those tough days.

Testimonials

"Definitely NOT your average coloring book." "I definitely recommend it"
-*Shay Smith, Owner of Salon Eleven*

"An excellent way to release stress and take your mind off of things"
-*Andrea Allwood, Claims Manager, Farmers Insurance*

"Informative yet very creative. I love it."
-*Laura Harris, Associate, Heatron Manufacturing*

"Brilliant idea, Tanasha Allwood." "You are a true blessing to others and I highly recommend this coloring book to everyone."
-*Lydia Garcia, Cashier, Wal-Mart*

"Something Different, yet unique."
-*Melinda DeCanter, Sales Associate, Michaels*

"I absolutely love your Buzzed Art Nite events and now I get to color some of those very same images." "Awesome." "I'm definitely going to enjoy this."
- *Crystal Adams, Fitness Instructor, YouFit*

"I heard adult coloring books can be very calming and relaxing. I sense Queendom all around you and will definitely be purchasing yours."
– *Mo Daley*

"Congratulations, I'm so excited for you and I love the book cover."
-*Tamika Conley*

Preface

The hope and desire with this book, is that you will use it as a tool to help you to wine down and relax at the end of a hectic and or stressful day, or even on days when you are not feeling like you are at your best, or perhaps days when you are feeling a bit sad or depressed. This book is designed enlighten you on art and its happiness effect. It is also designed to inspire you and elicit a more positive attitude and mental state of mind. Many times as adults, we use just words to express our thoughts, feelings and emotions. Often times we fail to realize that we are all the Picasso's of our own magnificent canvases or pages called life, and by being connected spiritually, we have the ability to color, draw, or paint a new masterpiece each day. Therefore, throughout this book there are actual art filled pages for you to allow your inner self-expressions to shine. Remember you are an artist, so grab some colored pencils or markers and have FUN!

Chapter 1
ART THERAPY

Before we dive into what exactly Art Therapy is, let me first start by saying, I initially discovered the concept of it about 4 years ago when I attended a corporate team-building event. There were about 20 of us women at this little tucked away art studio in Leawood, Kansas. There was food, drinks and games and an instructor who taught us all step-by-step how to paint a pretty sunflower. We each started out with our own blank canvas and had our own set of art supplies. At the end of the session, we each took turns going around the room saying something nice about our co-workers painting. I remember people laughing and having fun and forgetting all about the fact that we were at an off-site work event. Comradery had filled the room and we all seem less-stressed. It was that experience that truly left me with a sense of calmness that I had never felt before. I remember saying to GOD, "I'm going to own one of these little art studios someday".

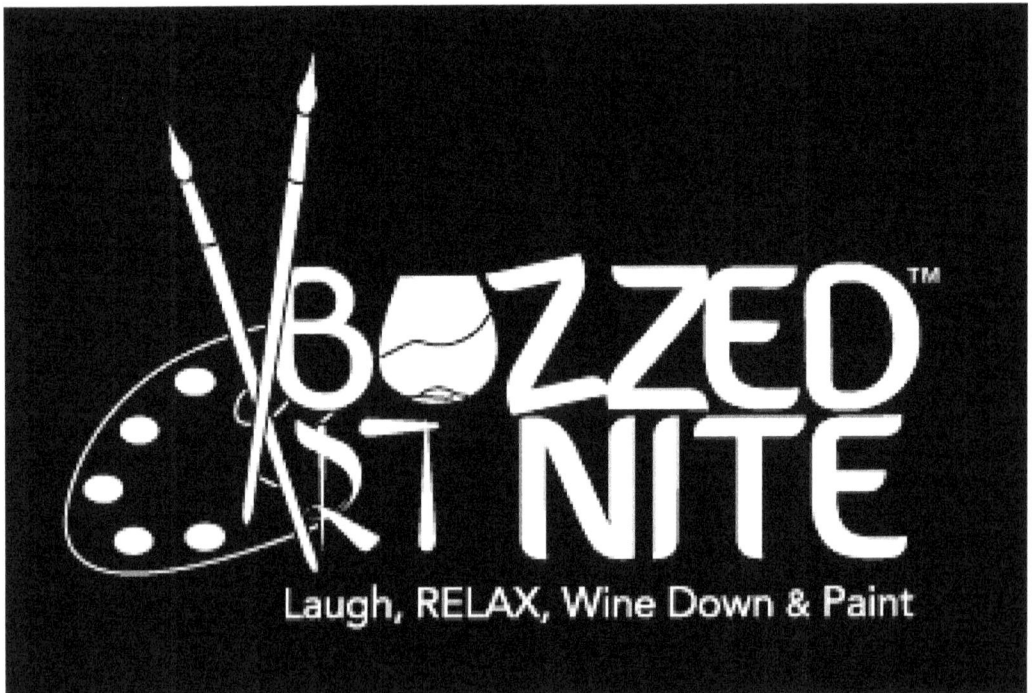

BUZZED™ ART NITE

Laugh, RELAX, Wine Down & Paint

Little did I know that HE was already working things out in my favor. You see sometimes in life; God has a way of moving us forward even when we do not want to nor do we understand why. I used to question God as to why certain things in my life were happening. I no longer question him nowadays as I find my purpose.

In February of 2014, I moved to Dallas, TX. I was not sure why until October of 2015 when I finally stepped out on faith and started my own wine and paint company called Buzzed Art Nite. I am believer that everything happens for a reason and I am so grateful that he put that desire in my heart several years ago and took me on this journey to be able to bless, inspire and educate others on art therapy.

Okay, so what exactly is Art Therapy you ask? Art Therapy is the releasing of the unconscious mind's thoughts by means of spontaneous art expression.

Art Therapy is a form of psychotherapy that allows the emotional expression and healing through non-verbal means.

Art Therapy primarily focuses on the visual arts such as coloring, painting, and drawing.

By creating visual works of art, and reflecting on the actual process and concentrating on the finished masterpiece, people can increase their own self-awareness, and the awareness of others.

With art therapy, people are also able to cope with symptoms of stress and anxiety much better.

Furthermore, they will be able to enhance their cognitive abilities and most importantly, they will enjoy the life-affirming pleasures of making art and feel more calm and relaxed.

Oprah Winfrey once said, "When you are not at ease with yourself and feeling all stressed out, that is how you know you are headed in the wrong direction. What you need to do is get still and relax".

Chapter 2

ART IS

Art itself comes in various forms such as music, dance, literature and painting.

Collectively, music, dance, literature and painting are known as the visual arts.

Visual arts are designed by the human creative mind too express and imagine and be admired for their beauty. The thing I love most about art is that it allows you to be yourself by expressing yourself. By making art that matters to you, you are in essence starting a conversation with everyone who sees it. You're saying, "Hey everyone, this is what matters to me. What do you think about it?"

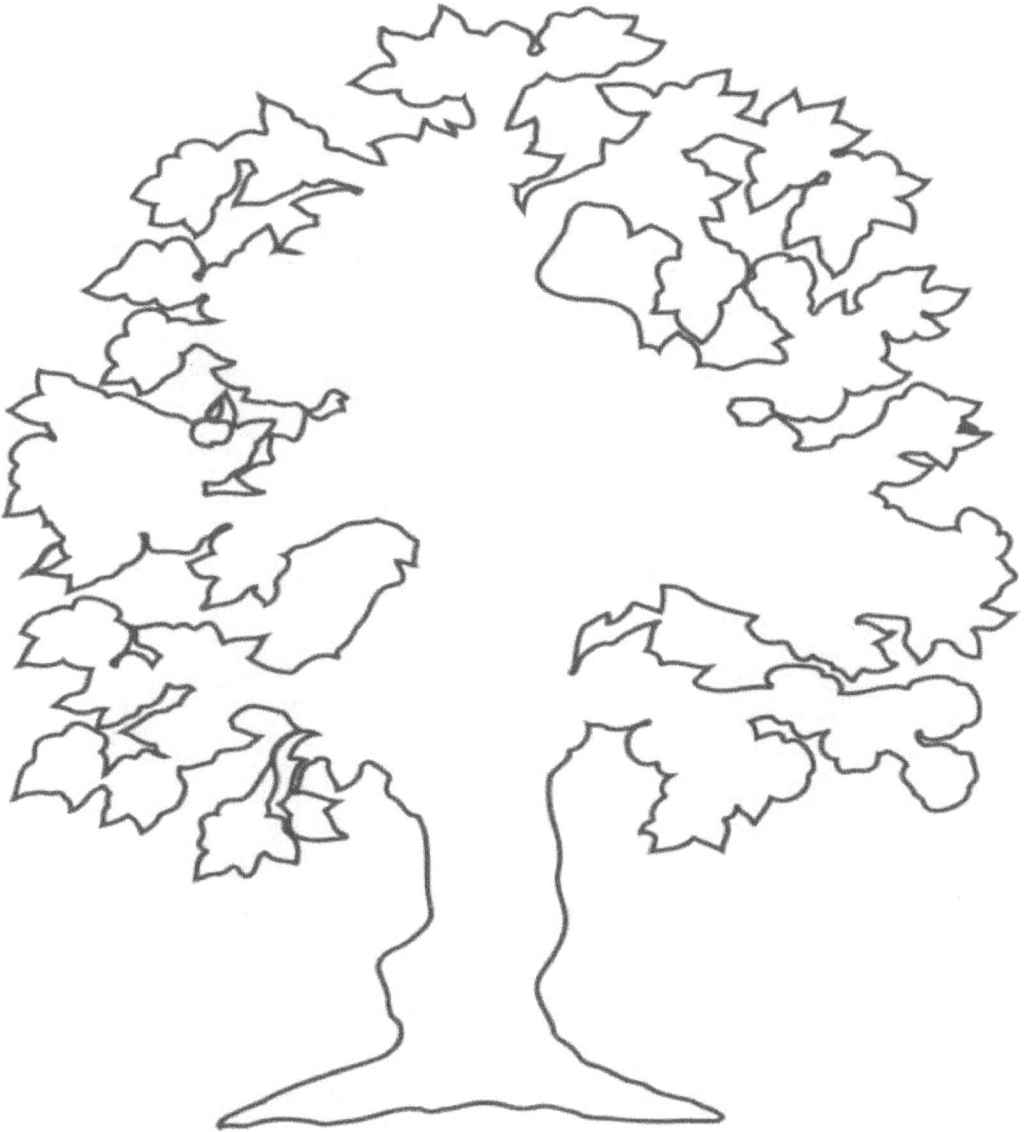

People ask me all the time, hey Tanasha, what makes your company different from some of the other wine and paint companies out there and I tell them, "I like creating artwork that others may actually be able to relate too somehow or be inspired by." "I like creating fun and hip artwork that is current in the world of pop-culture." For example, when PRINCE passed away, he had touched so many people's hearts and many folks were grieving his loss. However, with one of the paintings that was created at Buzzed Art Nite and inspired by PRINCE, people from all walks of life had the opportunity to come together and paint a masterpiece of him. The session allowed for dialogue, grieving, networking, socializing, and an overall fun, therapeutic experience and to me that's what art is.

Art is Appreciation
All the many things, I appreciate.
From the ups and downs,
to the TWISTs and turns
Like brush strokes on a canvas
I APPRECIATE

Art is Beautiful
oh that thing called LIFE,
Is oh so Beautiful
From a baby in a Womb
To the Heaven in the skies
Like a blank white canvas
To admiring the finished Masterpiece
My, oh my- that's BEAUTIFUL

Art is Creative
To the Earth, the Wind
And Adam and Eve
Piecing together all the vibrant colors
With all the designs and patterns
And all that matters
There's no denying, that Life & Art
Go Together
And oh how creative, and such a pleasure

Art is Different
All my Life
I have been the ONE
The one who is different, in the sistah's den
From the way I talk
To my pretty smile
Embracing all things Different
That's my style

Art is EMPOWERING
Sitting there starring
At the blank white canvas
Taking a deep breath
And with a brush in hand
Going full-speed ahead,
Amused and Amazed and
Saying to myself, Yeah, I did that.
Wow, how empowering Art can be

"When they go low, We Go High!"

Chapter 3
HAPPINESS

Happiness is a state of well-being and contentment. It is also a pleasurable satisfaction.

With each day that we are blessed to be on this beautiful earth, able to take in another deep breath of fresh air, enjoy a cup of tea, surround ourselves with true, supportive friends and loved ones,

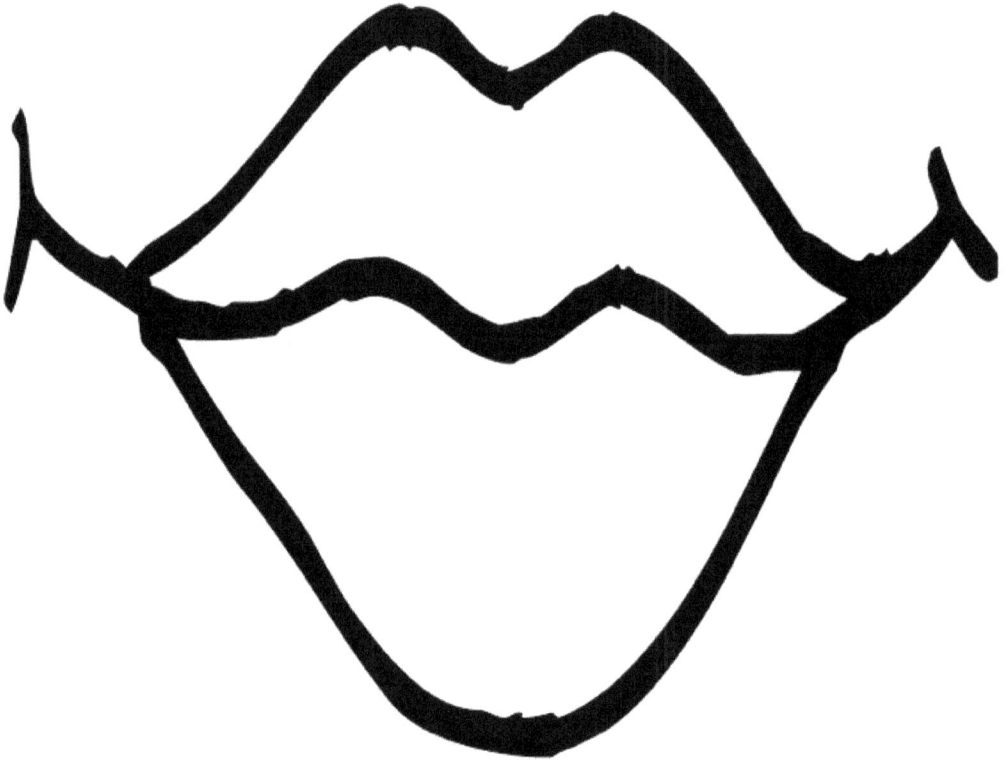

Or take in a quiet moment to be alone with our thoughts, or given the opportunity to try something fun and new like coloring, painting or drawing, or show our love for others and allow ourselves to be loved; that we are in essence experiencing happiness.

So when you think about happiness, really take a minute to step back and recognize all the good in your life.

Even if you have just a small glimmer of hope, do not discount it, that is happiness.

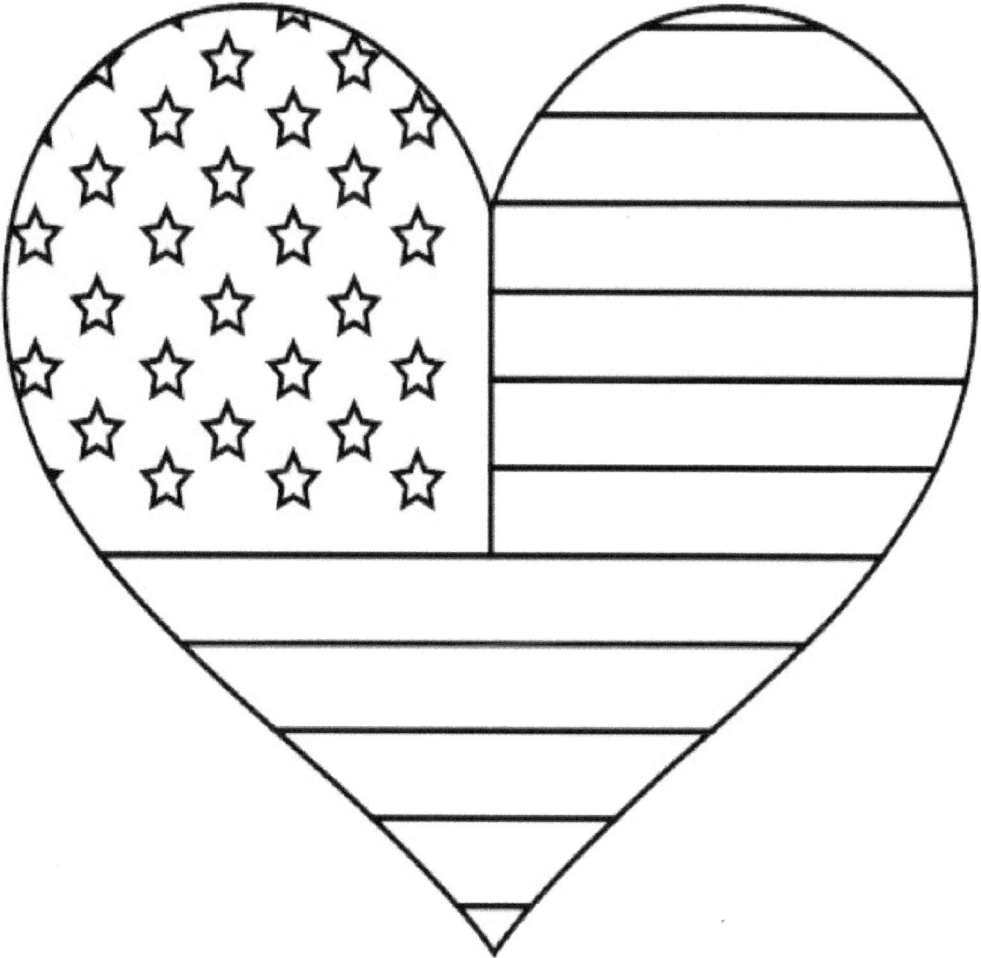

It is critical to remain positive and have a determination in your heart that sets your soul on fire. That determination is your passion.

Always pursue your passion, by doing so, you will reap the benefits of true happiness.

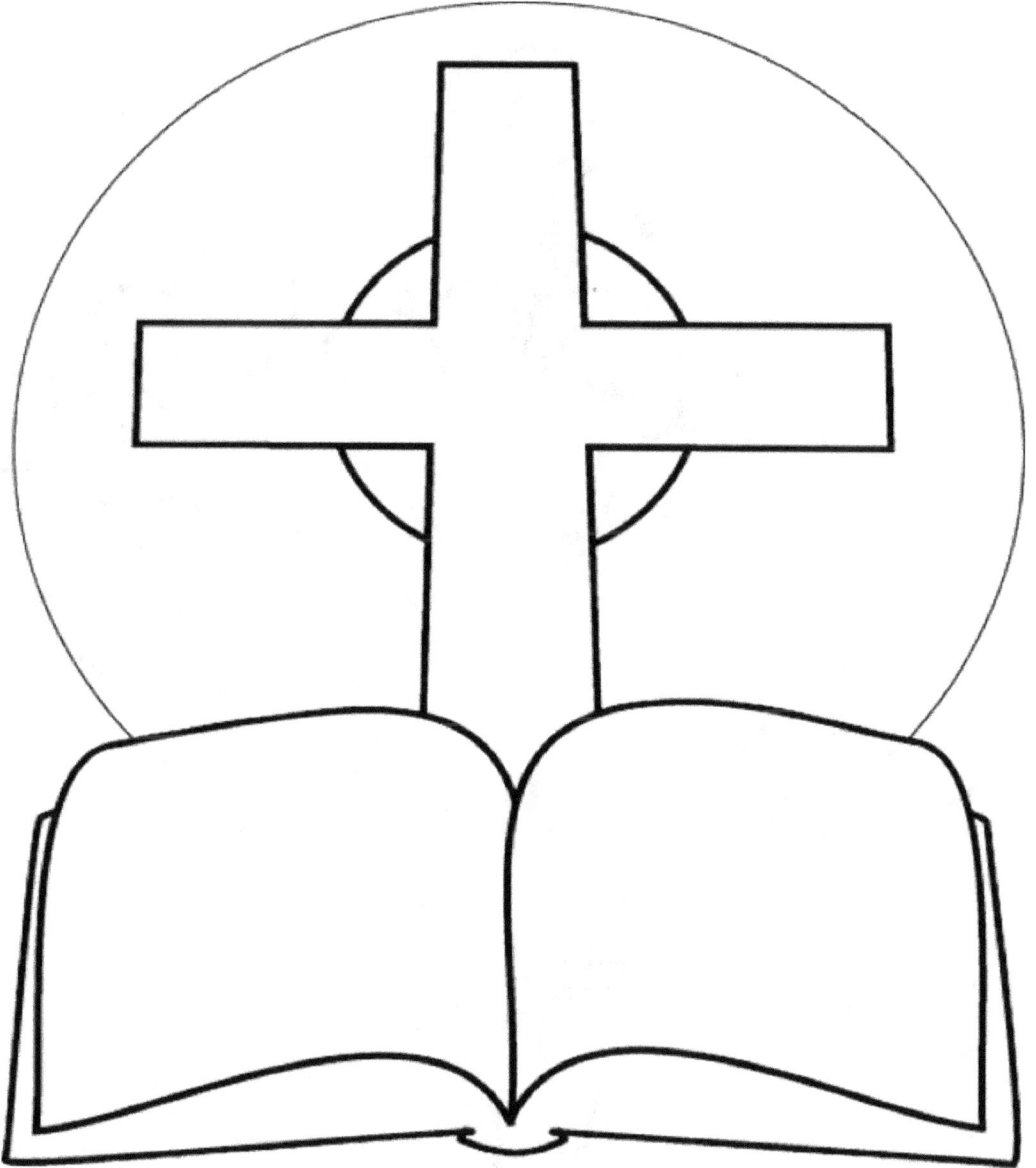

As you think about happiness, it is important to note that one must have faith and an unwavering spirit.

Faith is believing in the things that you cannot see. However, what you must do is listen to that inner voice.

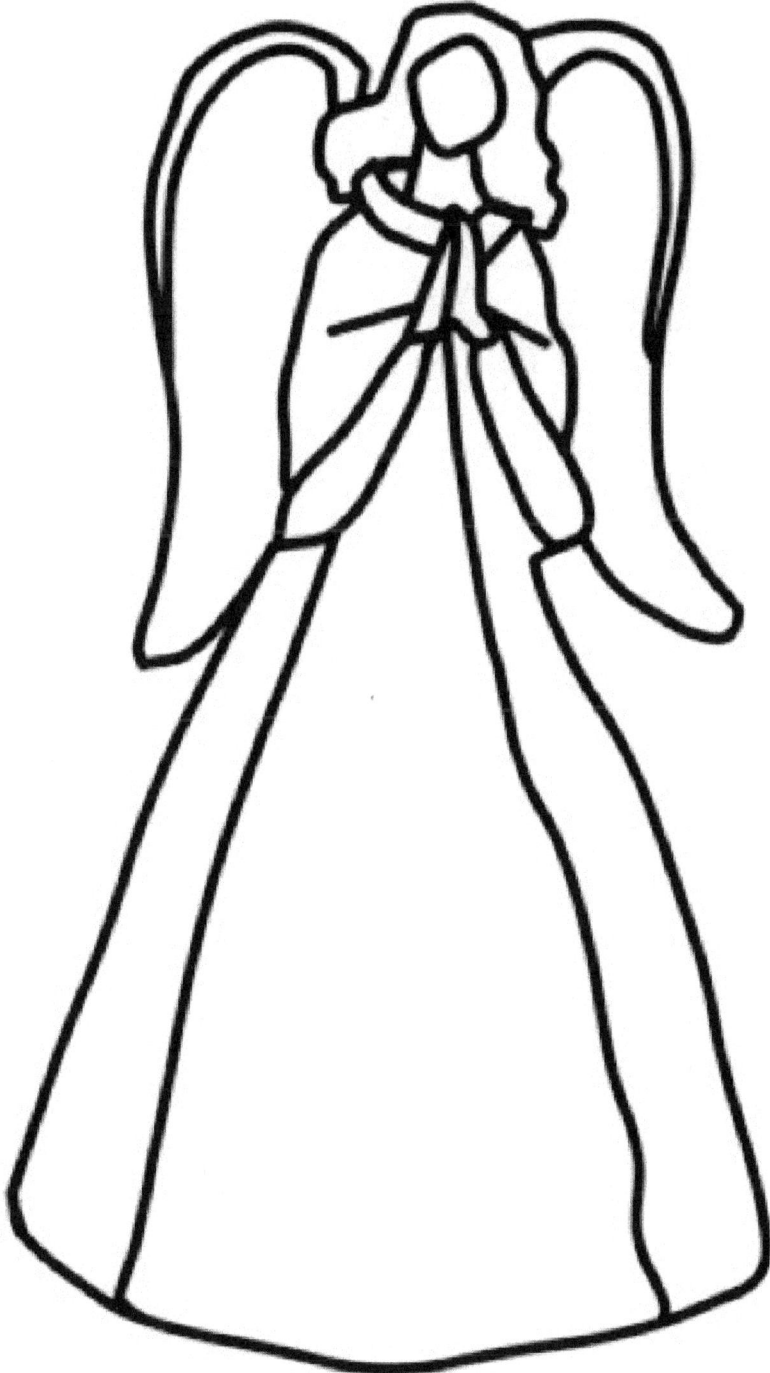

Listening to that inner voice, will lead you down a path of happiness.

And on the days when the going gets too tough, or the water appears to be too deep, and it seems as though the only choice you have is the one you are feeling,

Remember to look deep inside yourself and choose to see the possibilities instead. Choose love. Choose to help others.

Surround yourself with family and friends and get in the habitat of reciting positive affirmation and practicing positive self-talk.

Think about the good in your life and choose to live and be happy because after-all, happiness is a choice.

Elizabeth Gilbert once said, "Happiness is the result of your own personal efforts. It is something that you fight for, strive for, insist upon, and sometimes even travel around the world looking for it and that you must participate relentlessly because after-all, you are in charge of your own happiness".

I CAN DO all Things ~~~ Christ who STRENGTHENS Me

Chapter 4

STRESS MANAGEMENT

Did you know that Stressed spelled backwards spells Desserts?

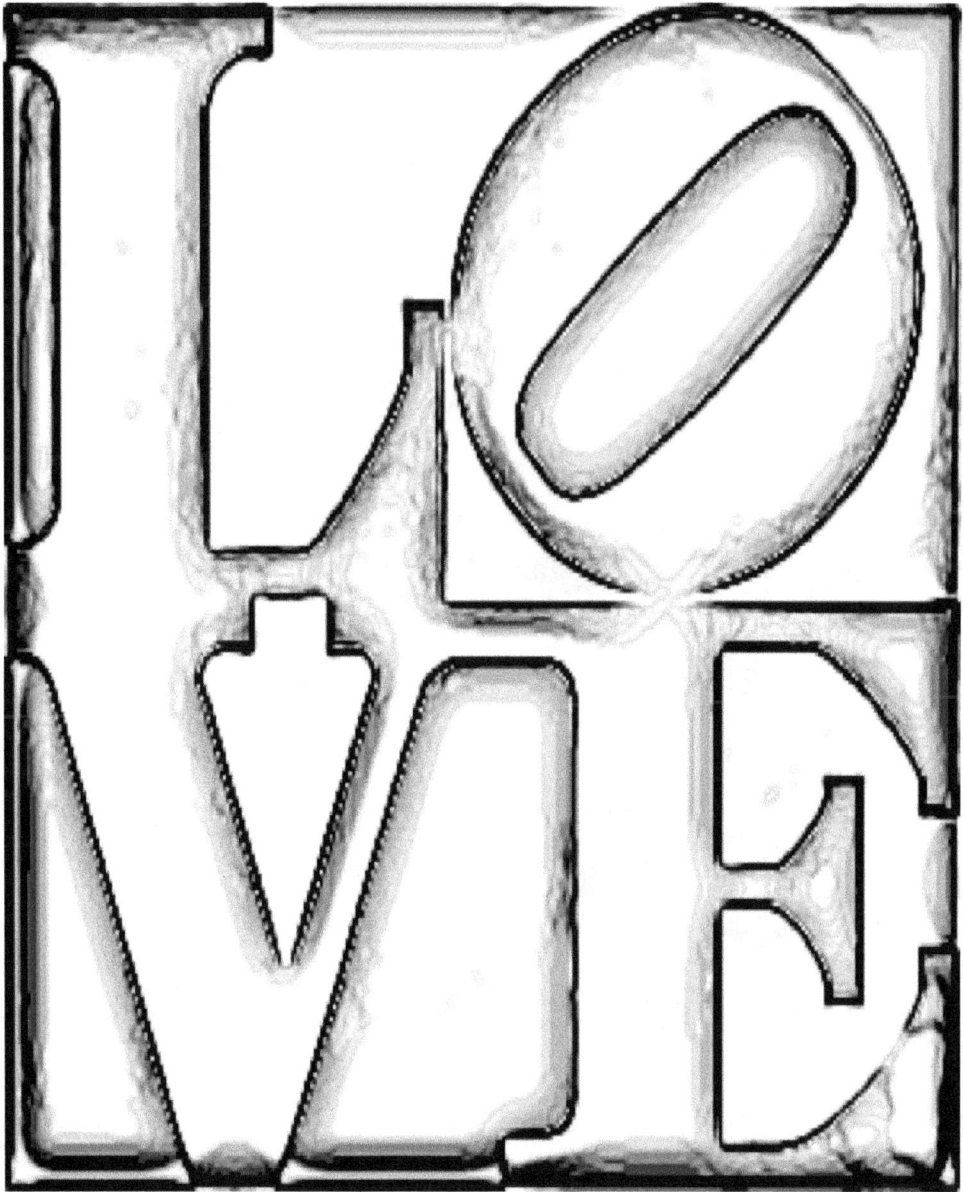

So what exactly is stress? Stress is any action or situation that upsets the body's normal equilibrium. Most people think of stress whenever their work-life and leisure demands exceed their ability to cope. Take a moment to think about all the stressors in your present life.

For many people, stress is defined differently. It could be weight gain, loss of a job or loved one, feelings of guilt and hopelessness, being frustrated and overwhelmed, dealing with family issues with a spouse or child, divorce, or my personal favorite placing too many high expectations upon ones-self.

Take a moment now and let your mind go by thinking of what your life would be like without stress.

Some thoughts that come to my mind immediately are joyful, peaceful and relaxing, happy and calm, wonderful and great, free to just be myself and live. What words or thoughts came to mind for you? Probably most of the same ones mentioned above. This book is meant to aid you with those happy thoughts. By allowing yourself to get still and relax your mind by coloring, you are able to manage your stress and achieve a greater state of peace and calmness.

I know for me; I absolutely love color. Color is the most important element of art. I like bright, bold colors like hot pink, royal purple, yellow, orange, and neon green. One of the things I always tell my artist that work for me, is to keep in mind that most people are attracted to bright bold colors so as we work together as a team to create artwork, let's always keep that in mind. To me there's no better way to express how you are feeling, or how you want someone else to feel, than through the use of color.

Did you know that Picasso painted for the sake of fulfillment and peace? Painting for him was something that soothed his soul. As a young kid, he was often told he had no talent. It was not until he fulfilled his need and desire to paint, that he discovered that others valued his fulfillment. I mention this story of Picasso because I can relate to it.

In July of 2015, my world as I knew it came crashing down on me once again. I was distraught, overwhelmed, frustrated, sad, depressed, stressed and suffering from anxiety. I was at yet another crossroad in my life that was all too familiar. I had been working in the field of Human Resources for the past 11 years of my life and just having a difficult time putting on that corporate face day in and day out. Often times, I appeared so stoic and withdrawn; I felt like I was losing my zest for life.

About 6 months prior to that, I had begun painting and coloring again. I was coming home from work in tears all the time. And the only real thing that seemed to sooth me was to have a glass of wine and paint or color. I would turn on some music and go to work. Although, it did not feel like work. It was fun actually. I was always relaxed afterwards not even realizing that hours had just passed by.

Also, many times while I was actually at work, I was closing my office door and just sitting there at my desk asking God, what is it? What do you have for me? What is my purpose? Why am I here? What am I good at? What's my talent? And then it just hit me in my dream one night. It was almost as if I heard a little whisper that said it's time.

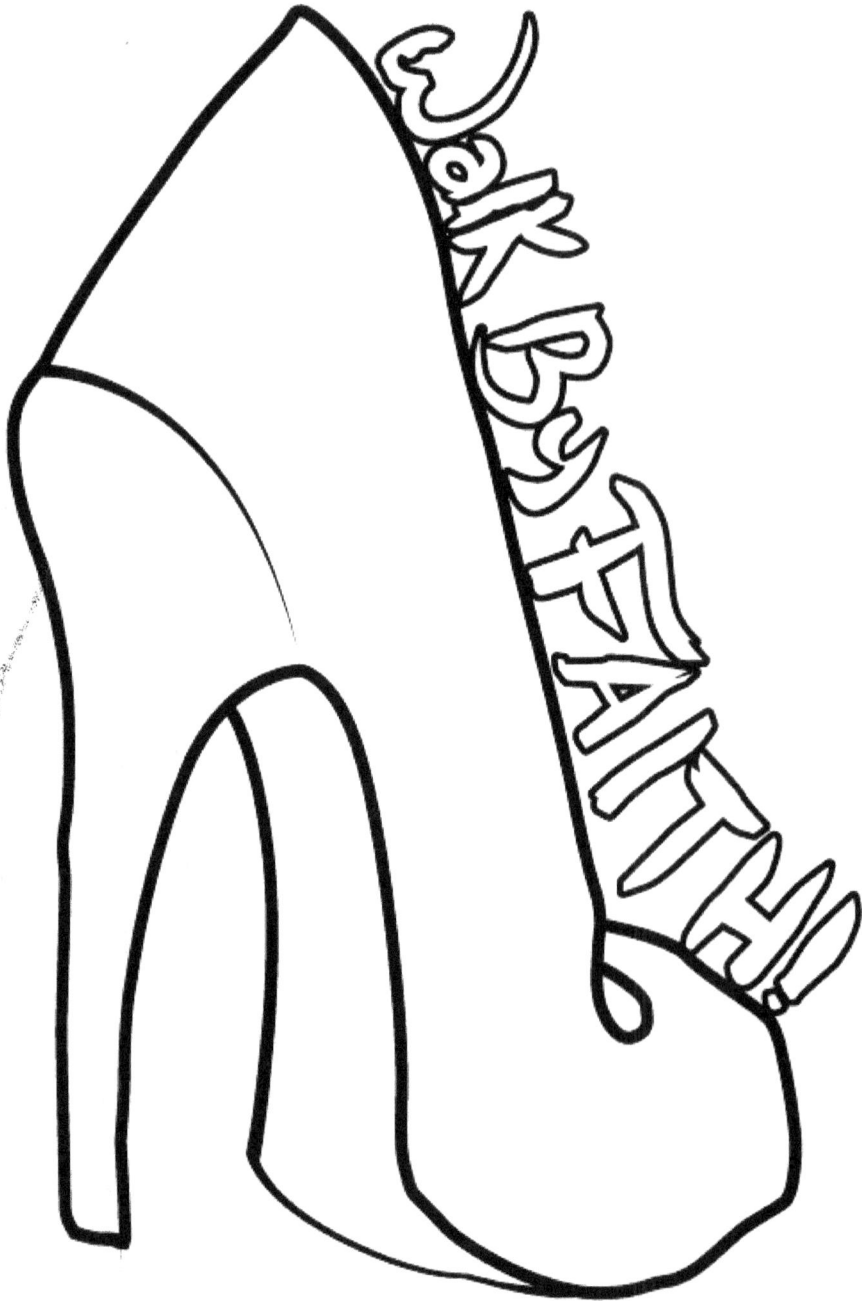

The next thing you know, I started going to church more and I was praying more and getting closer to GOD. I even joined the Greeters Ministry and started attending the Women's Ministry meetings. I was fasting more often and really just paying close attention to everything around me. I remember one Saturday afternoon I was re-organizing my knight-stand and I stumbled across a notepad of paperwork dated June 2012 and it said Buzzed Art.

At that very moment, a light bulb went off in my heart and my spirit. It was like an adrenaline rush. I was staying up late, waking up early. I had begun laying the groundwork to make what was once a dream, become my reality. And although at times I would still felt a little stress; it was now managed much better plus it was definitely overshadowed by my new found feelings of joy and happiness!

Now that you know what stress is let's consider for a moment how we can manage it. As mentioned before, coloring helps however knowing yourself and who you truly are, goes a long way as well in terms of your personality and how you choose to react to things. Chapter 5 touches on the importance of a positive attitude which is something that is key when dealing with stress and how you choose to react to it.

Some other ways to manage your stress is to ask yourself, will this matter in a year or two from now? If the answer is no, then let it go and do not let life circumstances control you; whether it be on your job, a dating relationship, and so on. Try to find a balance.

There are certain foods like sugar, caffeine, and salt can exaggerate your response to stress. Therefore, another great way to manage your stress is through diet and exercise. Both of which are areas of my life that I tend to struggle with but like anything else, it's a process and it takes time to break old habits.

Eating foods like fruits and vegetables will help reduce stress. Also, many people experience an emotional "high" after walking, running or even jogging. Exercise often provides experiences of relaxation and it helps the mind to look inward. Whenever your mind can relax and reflect, this undouble leads to a more sense of calm and reduced stress.

Let's switch gears and discuss anxiety. Anxiety is the fear of losing or having someone get ahead of you. Anxiety is commonly driven by the overly conscious of the criticisms and judgment of others. It is also per-petuated by unrealistic goals to be perfect. Take a moment to think about characteristics of people who may have anxiety and then take it a step fur-ther by relating this to your life presently. Are you suffering from anxiety?

Here are some common characteristics of someone with anxiety: Easily upset, worries a great deal, tense, agitated, nervous, fearful, and distressed. Here are some characteristics of someone not suffering from anxiety: Calm, relaxed, easygoing, patient, content, tranquil, and can deal with life one day at a time. Which one of these would you rather be? Hopefully you chose the latter of the two.

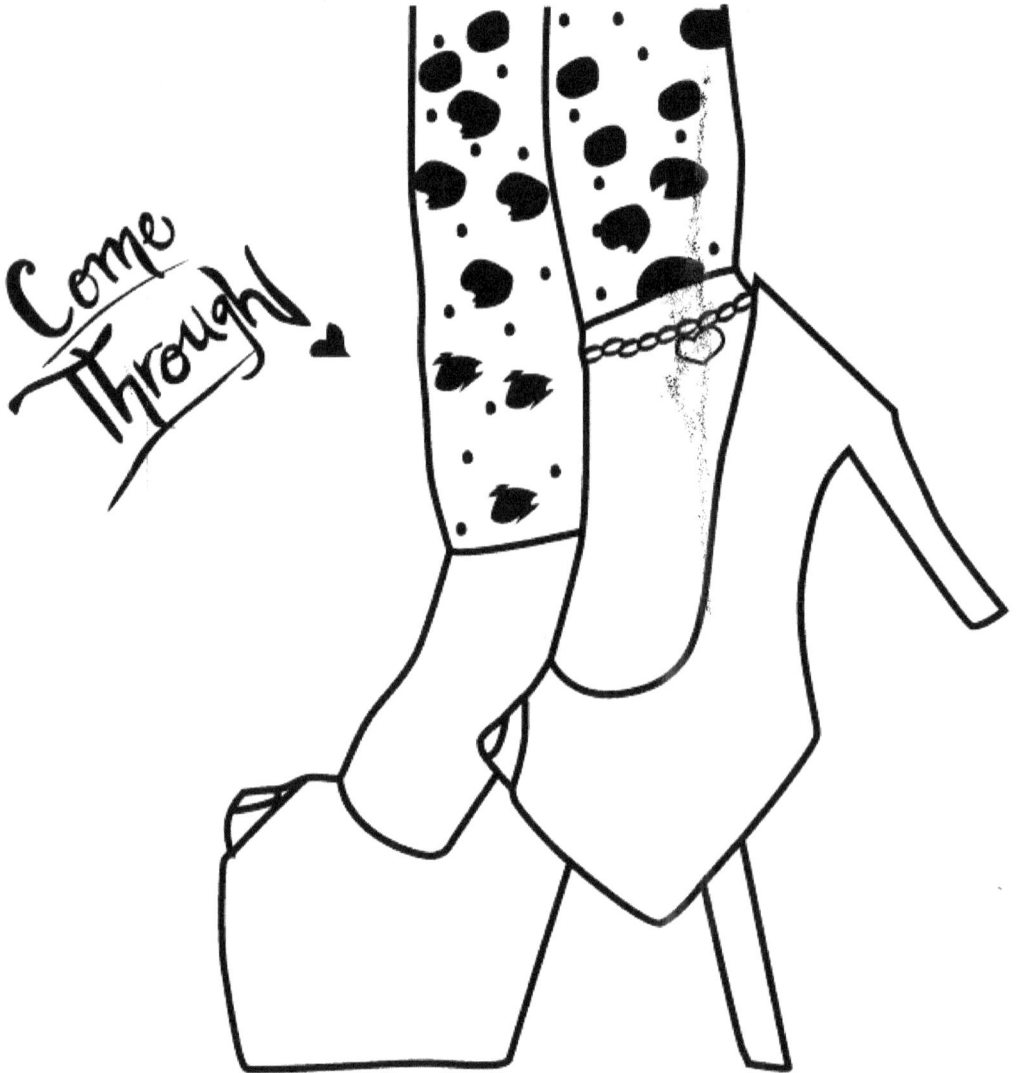

Again some form of exercise at least 20 minutes a day is recommended when combating anxiety. Not only that, but have you ever noticed how music helps you to feel more calm and relaxed? Often times when I am preparing a meal, painting or even coloring, I enjoy having some light music on in the background. I play songs that have meaning and elicit positive thoughts and emotions. Music helps get you to your happy place. As you color the next image, try listening to your favorite song.

Chapter 5

POSITIVE ATTITUDE

Attitude is a state of mind or feeling with regard to some matter. Attitude dictates whether you are living your life or if life is living you. Like the car keys used to start your car, having a positive attitude is the key to jump starting your life. Take a moment to really think about your attitude. Do you find yourself being on more of the positive side or more so on the negative?

Our choices boil down to two options when it comes to attitude. Negative or positive; and the great thing about them is that we get to choose which one will be our primary attitude. People that are referred to as optimistic are the people who have positive attitudes. On the flip side, people with negative attitudes are the pessimists. They have a tendency to suck all the life out of any situations. I like to call them FUNsuckers!

Now don't get me wrong. Optimistic people are not always 100% positive all the time. We have our down days every now and then. And pessimistic people can very well experience some bright sunny days as well. Again, it all goes back to how you choose to react to life that determines your outlook.

As your reading this book and coloring throughout the pages, let's say you identified mostly with being an optimistic person, to you I say, congratulations and keep up the happiness factor about yourself. But to those that struggle with pessimistic thoughts, I want to challenge you to take steps to change your behavior. 80% of life is all about our mental well-being and wherever your thoughts go, that is exactly where your energy goes.

Here are some steps that I have found has helped me throughout my life journey. Perhaps they will help you as well.

Step 1, whenever I am having a bad thought enter into my head, I take a moment and acknowledge it. Acknowledge that it is there, thank it for being there and then move on. This may sound simple to do, but many times as humans, we do not allow ourselves the time to just be alone with our thoughts, get still and relax. I am suggesting that even if you took just five minutes of your day whenever those negative thoughts begin to rear their ugly head into your mental space, acknowledge them and then move on; you'll see the world in a much more positive light.

For example, just the other day, as I was writing another chapter in this book; the thought entered my head and said, "Why are you writing this book?" "Who's going to buy it?" I acknowledge those thoughts, thanked them and let them go. Later that day, as I was scrolling through my social media feed on Facebook, there were two women who made a comment about purchasing an adult coloring book because it's very relaxing and calming. As I read that post and smiled, I thanked GOD. That post was meant for me to see. It was my validation to keep going forward with my book project.

Kim Vance once said, "Create what sets your soul on fire and it will illuminate the path ahead."

Step 2 is to focus on what you can and cannot control in your life. One of the mantras that I like to repeat to myself is, "Let it go, and let GOD". Now say this to yourself, "Let it go, and let God". Try to get in the habit of repeating this mantra or creating your own and repeating to yourself at least right before you go to bed or the first thing when you wake up. Studies show that our subconscious mind is most receptive during those times.

In the past I use to be a very controlling person and I have found that it was due to fear, a lack of trust, and lack of faith. Living like that brought on a great deal of unnecessary stress. It wasn't until I began repeating various mantras that I learned to have faith, trust in the lord, and really understood what fear was. From there I started noticing that I had actually begun to "Let it go, and let God". I believe that because of this new habitat; that I became much more positive and happier, less stressed, calm and relaxed and less controlling and found my joy.

The last key step is to talk to a supportive person about how you feel. I used to be someone that would bottle things up inside and let things fester. I would withdraw from meetings and conversations and overall just isolate myself into this bubble because I felt so misunderstood. The problem with that, is that it was not healthy. Fast forward to today, I have no issue with sharing how I feel and I no longer allow things to fester. I don't enjoy that bubbled up feeling like I'm about to explode so when things bother me, I talk about it, I let it flow and then I move on and I feel much better.

Chapter 6

INSPIRATIONAL QUOTES

One of the things that I enjoy doing is reading positive and inspirational quotes. Sometimes I take pictures of them so that I can be reminded of the words. Sometimes I write them down on a sticky note and hang them up on the mirror in my bathroom. I also keep a daily gratitude journal and often times, if I am attending a women's empowerment brunch, or a networking seminar, I love to jot down things that resonate with me and refer back to as I keep pushing forward with this journey called life.

Therefore, the next few pages of the book are comprised of various inspirational quotes. Take some time to read through each of the quotes and of course color the pages. Again, this is a section that you can always refer back to if you need just a quick pick me up. Not only that, I encourage you to perhaps think of some of your own inspirational quotes and like me, jot them down on paper, refer to them often and get in the habit of keeping a gratitude journal. I believe you will truly find this will make a world of difference in keeping you calm, relaxed, and stress-free.

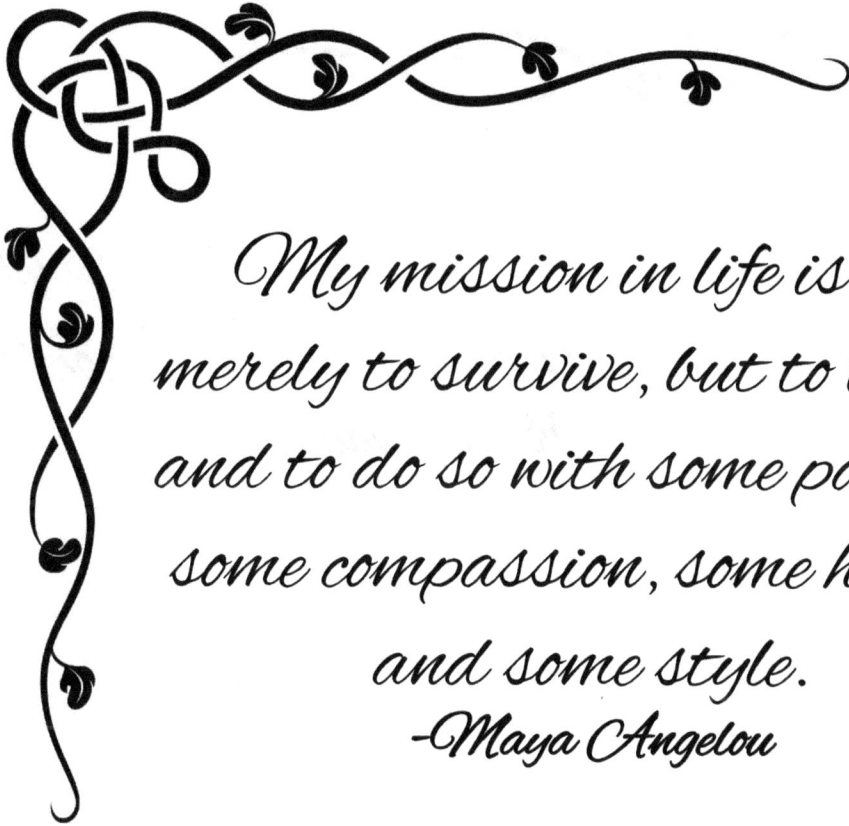

My mission in life is not merely to survive, but to thrive, and to do so with some passion, some compassion, some humor and some style.
-Maya Angelou

There is Nothing More truly artistic than to Love People.
-Vincent Van Gogh

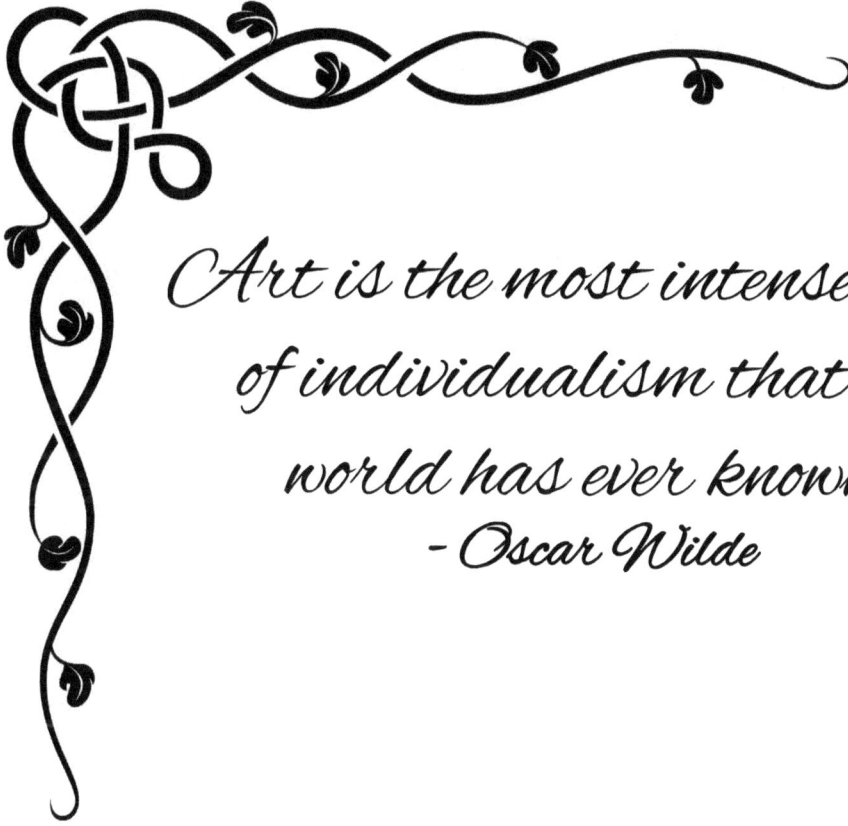

Art is the most intense mode of individualism that the world has ever known.
- Oscar Wilde

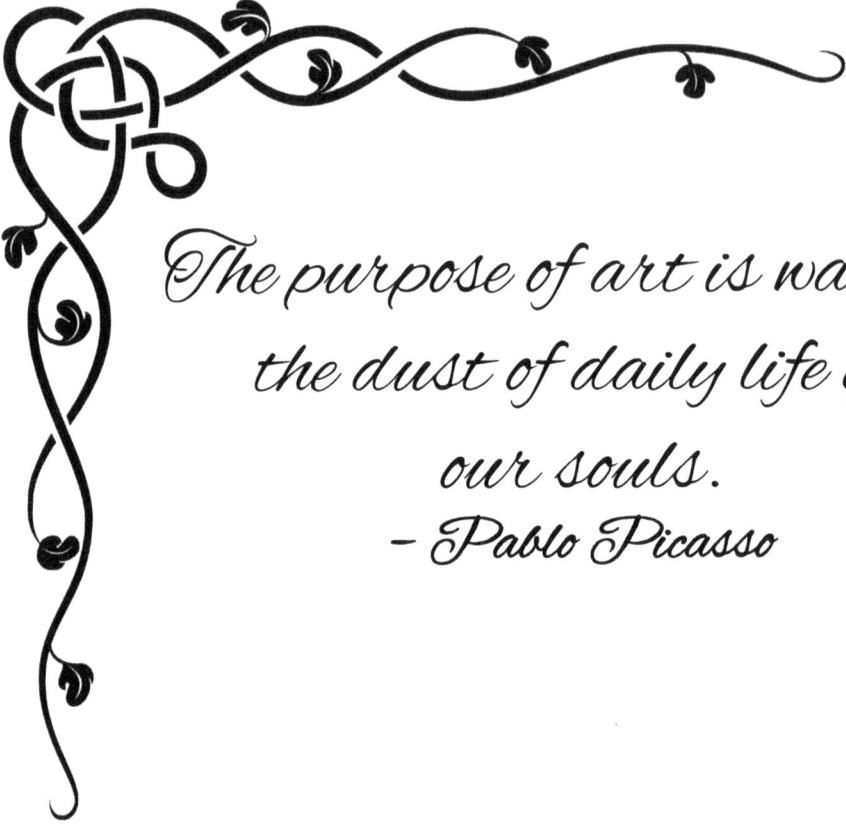

The purpose of art is washing
the dust of daily life off
our souls.
– Pablo Picasso

The aim of art is to represent not the outward appearance of things, but their inward significance.

– Aristotle

Filling a space in a beautiful way, that's what art means to me.

— Georgia O'Keeffe

*You Only Live Once
(YOLO)*

- Drake

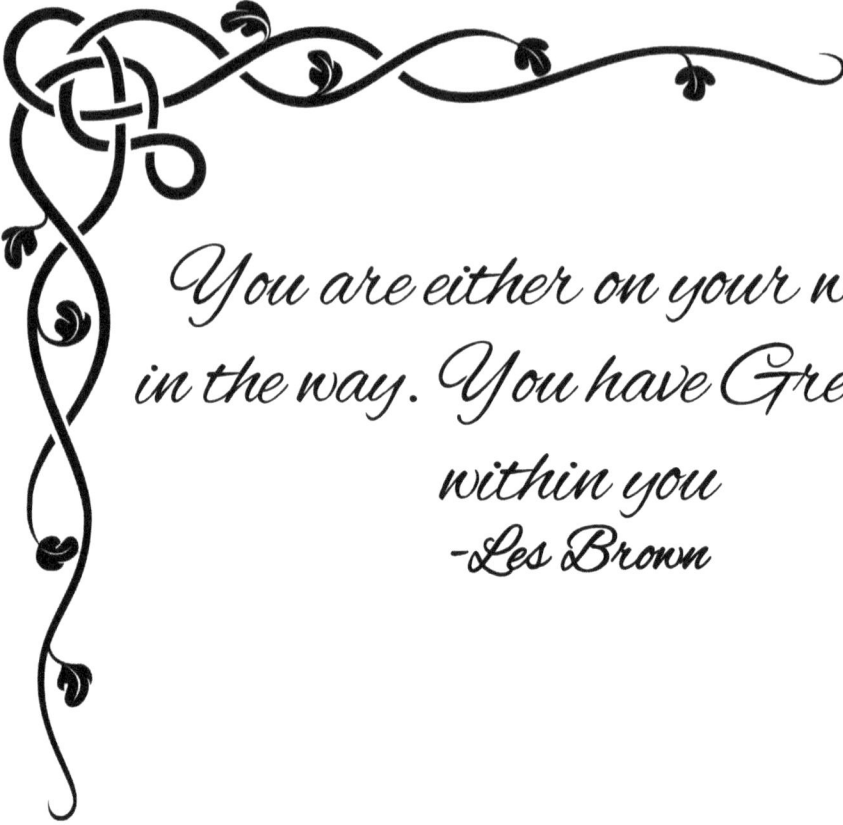

You are either on your way or in the way. You have Greatness within you
-Les Brown

Color today so great, that you make yesterday jealous

-Tanasha Allwood

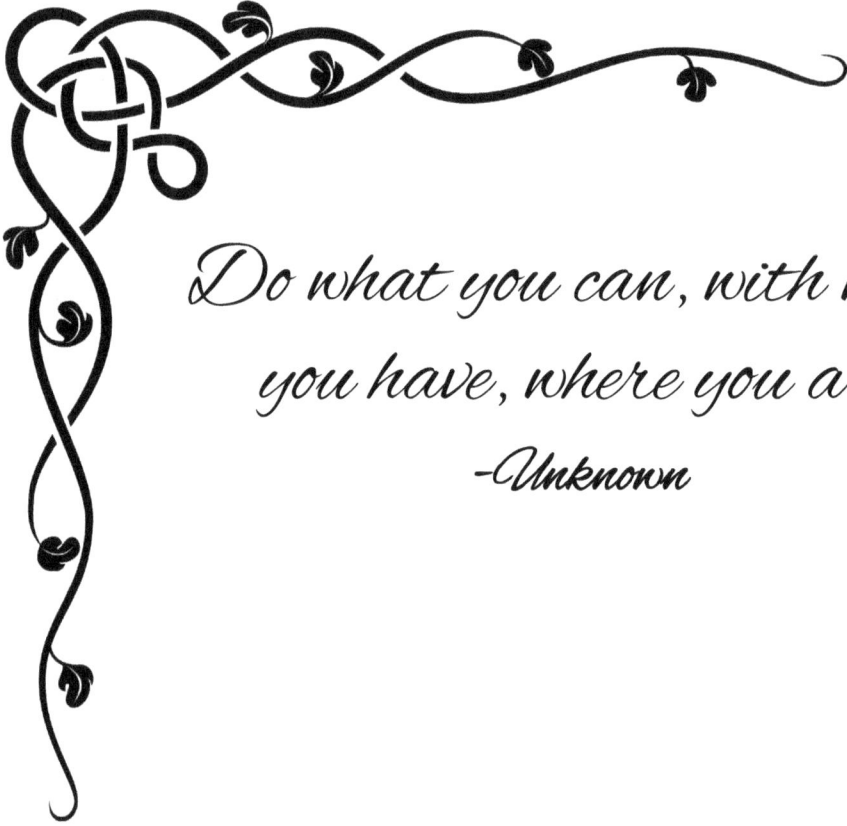

Do what you can, with what you have, where you are

-Unknown

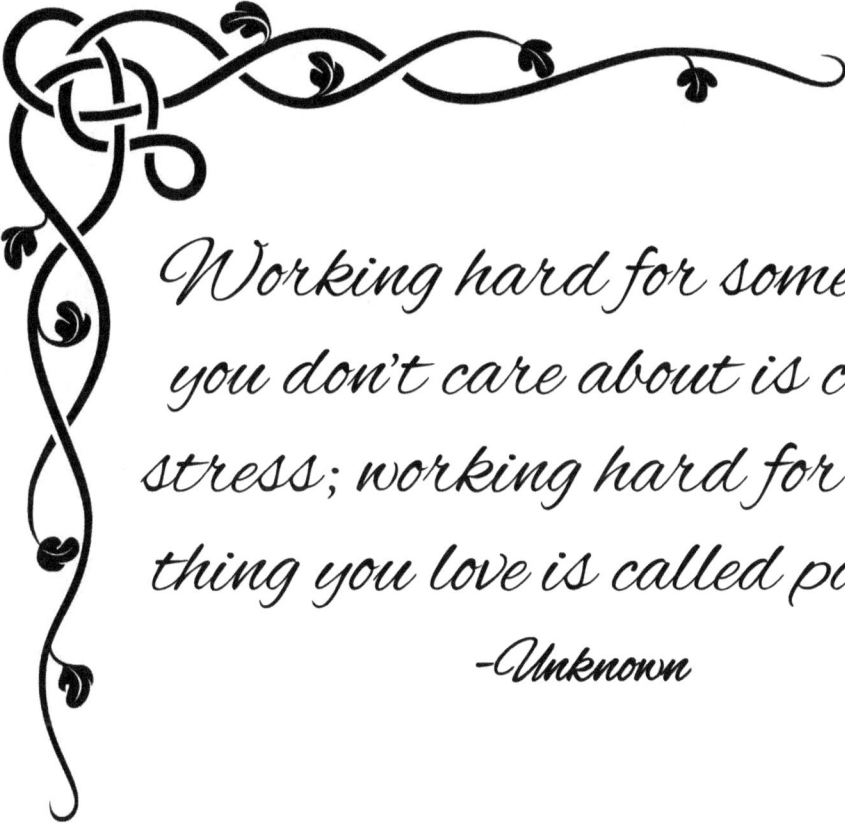

Working hard for something you don't care about is called stress; working hard for something you love is called passion

-Unknown

This one is my personal favorite: Trust in the Lord with all your heart and lean not on your own understanding; in all your ways acknowledge him, and he will direct your path.
- Proverbs 3:5-6 NKJV

Life is a great big canvas, and you should throw all the paint on it you can.

- Danny Kaye

Color is a power which directly influences the soul..
- Wassily Kandinsky

Timing is Everything. If it's meant to happen, it will and for the right reason
-Power of Positivity

As you color in your last page of this book, I'd like to take the time to thank you for your support by purchasing this adult coloring book. Hopefully, you will have been inspired to continue or improve upon living a life that is more calm and relaxed and stress-free. We talked about art therapy and what it is and how you can use it in your daily life. Art itself can mean many different things to different people and I encourage you to continue to think about what art means to you and how each day you are blessed to see another day, that is your opportunity to start with that blank page and color it great. Make a choice to keep a positive attitude about life and keep your stress at bay in order to maintain a healthy balance. Be encouraged and inspired by the various inspirations around you whether it be quotes, mantras, music, poems and so on. And by any means necessary, keep the faith and follow your passions, for they will lead you to your purpose! Speaking of which, anytime you're interested in attending a public wine and paint event or hosting a private wine and paint party definitely choose Buzzed Art Nite, LLC. Our website is **www.buzzedartnite.com**.

Thank you and God Bless!

www.ingramcontent.com/pod-product-compliance
Lightning Source LLC
Chambersburg PA
CBHW062050090426
42740CB00016B/3081